RING OF EARTH

A CHILD'S BOOK OF SEASONS

This ring of earth, this world, this sphere, enclosed within the circled year.

BY JANE YOLEN

ILLUSTRATED BY JOHN WALLNER

HARCOURT BRACE & COMPANY

San Diego   New York   London

Requests for permission to make copies of
any part of the work should be mailed to:
Permissions Department, Harcourt Brace & Company,
6277 Sea Harbor Drive, Orlando, Florida 32887-6777.

Library of Congress Cataloging-in-Publication Data.

Yolen, Jane.

Ring of earth.

Summary: The four seasons are viewed in poetry
from the perspective of a weasel, spring peeper, dragonfly, and goose.
1. Children's poetry, American.
2. Seasons—Juvenile poetry. 3. Animals—Juvenile poetry.
[1. Seasons—Poetry. 2. Animals—Poetry 3. American poetry]
I. Wallner, John, ill. II. Title.
PS3575.O43R5 1986   811'.54   86-4800
ISBN 0-15-267140-4

Printed in the United States of America
C D E F G

The art in this book was created with watercolor paints
and colored pencils on Fabriano 100-lb. watercolor paper.

The text and display type was set in Minister Light
by Central Graphics, San Diego, California.

Color separations were made by Heinz Weber, Inc.,
Los Angeles, California.

Printed by the Eusey Press,
Leominster, Massachusetts

Bound by The Book Press,
Brattleboro, Vermont

Production supervision by Warren Wallerstein

Designed by Michael Farmer and Dalia Hartman

". . . the Power of the World always works in circles . . ."

—Black Elk

for John Gregory Yolen,
with love

—J. Y.

for Elmas Ohnigian:
the ring continues

—J. W.

WINTER SONG OF THE WEASEL

The nose knows. I hunt the wind.
In summer I breathe sun-plumped skin
of rabbits resting in a hole;
or blindly sweet inviting mole;
or the musky summer frog
that squats upon a saucer log
and beckons with its muddy smell.
Oh, summer scents I know full well.
But winter . . .

Then I use a different track.
Casting forward, casting back,
I sniff the rising hump of land
beneath a towering maple stand.
And then from pine trees tipped with snow
comes the scolding of a crow
who punctuates his winter rage,
a comma, black on winter's page.
And just beyond, dead timothy
sends shaky signals back to me.
My ring of teeth ache with the fear
that I won't know when food is near
in winter.

Winter fields wear smocks of snow
disguising all who sleep below
in caves and warrens, dens and lairs,
the wintering of 'chucks and bears
whose dreams are fat and dark and deep.
They make their living out of sleep.
Winter ponds wear skins of bright
hardened ice that shows no light.
I see no fish beneath that sheen.
What was once cannot be seen
in winter.

And so I change.
I reproduce upon my hide
the wintering I feel inside.

For I was dark and now am light.
For I was brown and now am white.
For I was summer, now am snow.
Upon my back the seasons grow.
And—once again—I know.

SONG OF THE SPRING PEEPER

All winter long I slept below
A quilt of moss and bark and snow
Till the steady drip of melt beat down
Exposing undersheets of brown.
Now birds wing north with naught to do
Until *I* give the spring its cue.

Pe-ep. Pe-ep. Pe-ep. Pe-ep.

On a solitary bough the redwing sings,
But few the changes that blackbird rings.
No rising moon, no brand-new breeze
Are called up by *his* squawking pleas.
He claims his space, his place, his air,
For none but blackbirds does he care.

Pe-ep. Pe-ep. Pe-ep. Pe-ep.

And who else waits? Bears new awoke,
Meandering; the mourning cloak
A-flutter in a warming breeze;
And on the graying banks, snow fleas;
And little nymphs, brief bound-up lives,
Upon whose flesh the trout survives.
Violets first, then ferns unfold,
And trilliums ignore the cold
That lingers just a day or two
Before the world springs up anew.

Pe-ep. Pe-ep. Pe-ep. Pe-ep.

The nights grow shorter, the days grow long,
But the beat of the world is the beat of my song.
Do you see the moss and the fiddlehead frond?
Like bullhead lily or the ripples in the pond,
They are merely settings for the tune I sing
As up from the edge of the world I bring
                                        SPRING!

Pe-ep. Pe-ep. Pe-ep. Pe-ep.

But where does spring start? In the throat.
The high sweet chirp, a single note
That pipes through swamp, across the pond,
To reed-edged banks and fields beyond,
Past woods, to towns, to—the edge of the world.

And there . . . and there is spring unfurled.

My song. *My* gift. *My* world. *My* spring—
And all I have to do is sing.

Pe-ep. Pe-ep. Pe-ep. Pe-ep.

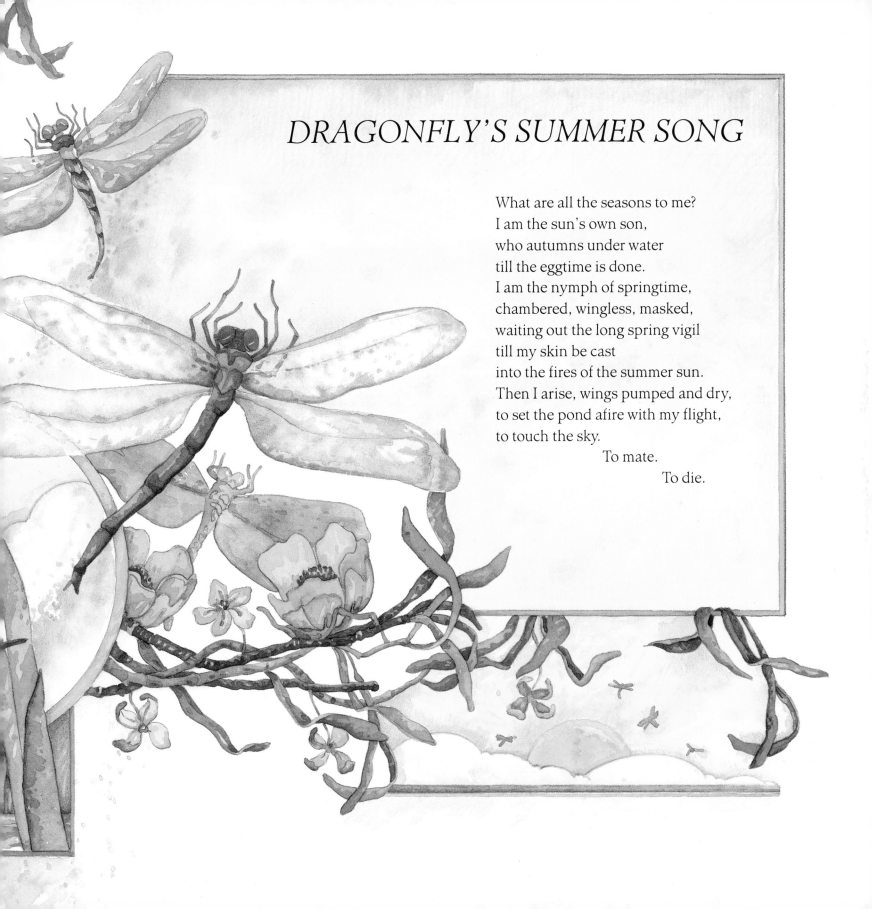

DRAGONFLY'S SUMMER SONG

What are all the seasons to me?
I am the sun's own son,
who autumns under water
till the eggtime is done.
I am the nymph of springtime,
chambered, wingless, masked,
waiting out the long spring vigil
till my skin be cast
into the fires of the summer sun.
Then I arise, wings pumped and dry,
to set the pond afire with my flight,
to touch the sky.
       To mate.
           To die.

I am the sun's own darling.
My wings catch the flame.
Darning needle, Doctor, Hawk,
Dragon's Dragon is my name.
I was here at world's first turning,
I will be here at the last.
What are the swift seasons to me
whose father's father's father knew the past?

I am the wind's own stepchild,
wings colorless as air,
veins like stained glass ribbings
trapping all the sun's light there.
I am day's own champion,
gladiator, knight,
ready at the summer's dawning
for a voracious fight.

                Or flight.

I am the summer's dandy,
I am swiftness, I am light,
I am the reaper of the pond,
I am death in winged flight.
What to me the world below
where water striders pace the pond,
or world above where vees of geese
honk for a moment, then are gone?
I was here at world's first turning,
I will be here at the last.
What are the swift seasons to me
whose father's father's father knew the past?

AUTUMN SONG OF THE GOOSE

Rise up, rise up, my mate,
from the chilly land,
for a rich, warm smell
as subtle as a poem
rides the air
and calls us home.

Kerhonk. Kerhonk. Kerhonk.

Rise up, rise up, my friends,
from the dying land
where the headless stalks
of flowers bend
in their earthen tombs
and there are left but a few
of summer's brittle blooms.

Kerhonk. Kerhonk. Kerhonk.

The sun hangs between mountains,
the air is crisp and cold.
It is the time of flight.
Rise up, rise up, my mate, my friends,
into the piercing light.
Along the road of air
where the strong winds blow,
along the gray tunnel
lit by the pale moon,
gray sky above,
gray mud below,
and the long winds singing
their mournful old tune.
Then down to the lake
to keep our feet warm.
Nibble and shake,
nibble and shake,
a few more miles across autumn
a few more miles safe
from winter's cold alluring charm.

Kerhonk. Kerhonk. Kerhonk.

Into shallow sleep we fall,
while all about
the lullaby call
murmurs across the changing land.
Even in sleep
night whispers its warnings:
fox and stoat,
and the hunter with his gun,
blindly waiting in the early mornings.

Rise up, rise up, my friends,
and mount the singing air.
Over the changing autumn fields,
past ponds veiled in mists.
Past trackless mountains
where the trees rise up like fists.
Past houses, past towns
where small people live small lives.
It is morning, my mate,
my friends. Rise up. Rise.

Kerhonk. Kerhonk. Kerhonk.

We fly but wingtips apart,
No compass, no compass but the heart.

Kerhonk. Kerhonk. Kerhonk.

AUTHOR'S NOTE

In the winter, the weasel or stoat sheds its summer coat, and its brown body becomes white, all except for a black tip of tail. This is a response to the seasonal change in the light. A successful predator, the weasel will eat anything from frogs to mammals larger than itself. It is noted for its sharp ring of 34 teeth and the fact that once it sinks its teeth into something, it never lets go.

The spring peeper is a tiny one-inch pond frog whose insistent trillings—a round of four double-syllabled peeps—are often the first recognizable sign of spring. Other signs include bears up from their winter sleep, the appearance of the mourning cloak butterfly, snow fleas that dust the banks of old snow, and, in the melting ponds, the nymphal or larval stage of insects such as the dragonfly. Early spring flowers also call attention to the fact that the northern hemisphere is tilting toward the sun, and days are growing longer, nights shorter. But for many rural folk it is the song of the peeper that really heralds the new spring.

The dragonfly's brief winged life—it lives in or under the water in its first two stages, egg and nymph—is an ironic commentary on its role in the history of life on earth. The earliest known dragonfly fossils are from the late Carboniferous period of 300 million years ago. And dragonflies almost identical to modern dragonflies were fossilized during the Jurassic period, 150 million years ago, making them contemporaries of the giant dinosaurs.

The goose mates for life and flies in great groups, winging south during the late autumn. The long migratory patterns take vees of geese over most of the world—across continents and over oceans. The internal "compass" that guides them is complex, having to do with all their senses, wind-carried clues, and star and ground patterns. We do not understand it very well.

21569

J
811   Yolen, Jane.
YOL
          Ring of earth.

$14.95

J
811   Yolen, Jane.
YOL   21569
                Ring of earth.

$14.95

DATE	BORROWER'S NAME	
SEP 1 9 199_	Heeln Natasha A	
APR 2 9 199_	Tomisha Benna	